Original title:
Petal Pursuits

Copyright © 2025 Creative Arts Management OÜ
All rights reserved.

Author: Sebastian Whitmore
ISBN HARDBACK: 978-1-80566-691-2
ISBN PAPERBACK: 978-1-80566-976-0

Blossoms as Messengers of Hope

In the garden's bright glaze,
Blooms giggle and sway,
They whisper sweet secrets,
Chasing worries away.

With a wink and a grin,
They promise the sun,
Even rain can't dampen,
Their joy has begun.

Dance of the Wildflowers

Wildflowers in a row,
Jive to the breeze,
Twisting and turning,
They're the dance floor tease.

Bees bust a move,
Buzzing with flair,
While ants on the ground
Are giddy with care.

Embracing the Garden's Essence

In the sun's warm embrace,
Plants share their delight,
With petals like giggles,
They cheer up the night.

Frogs croak in harmony,
A chorus of cheer,
While snails in their shells
Are just glad they're here.

Petals Like Time: A Seasonal Tale

Spring sprinkles the earth,
With colors so bright,
While summer's all laughter,
And tickles goodnight.

Autumn wears a crown,
Of leaves in a whirl,
And winter giggles softly,
At snow's magic swirl.

The Art of Seasonal Discoveries

In springtime's dance, I trip and fall,
Chasing blooms, I hear them call.
A daffodil whispers with glee,
"Catch me quick, if you can, whee!"

Under a sun that darts and plays,
I spot a flower, oh, what a phase!
Turns out it's a weed, much to my dread,
Guess I'll just hug my garden shed.

Capturing the Silken Touch of Spring

I stumbled soft on grass so green,
Hoping to catch the floral sheen.
A butterfly laughed as it flew by,
"Nice try, my friend, but that's not high!"

With paint and brush, I gave it a whirl,
Trying to capture that springtime swirl.
But art that sways just like a breeze,
Left me grinning, laughing with ease.

Embracing the Garden's Rhapsody

In my garden, with joy I jumped,
But who knew a cactus had me thumped?
As laughter erupted from my right knee,
The roses said, "That's quite a spree!"

The daisies giggled, swaying along,
My purple socks clashed, oh so wrong!
Yet in this mess, I found my cheer,
For every thorn, there's laughter near.

Beneath a Canopy of Colors

Beneath the arch of colorful hues,
The bees whizzed by, giving me clues.
"Dance with us, oh lady of grace,
Unless you trip, then there's no race!"

With laughter ringing, I joined their flight,
My shoes untied, oh what a sight!
Yet in this chaos, blossoms would sing,
For every tumble, comes spring's zing!

Secrets of the Daisy Chain

In the garden, oh what a sight,
Daisies giggle from morning till night.
They whisper secrets to every bee,
"Don't step on me, or you'll spill your tea!"

Buttercups join in with a twirl,
Claiming each petal is a precious pearl.
"Every flower has its own tale to tell,"
They chuckle together, wishing all well.

A Lullaby of Floral Echoes

Sunflower sways, a dancer in glee,
Waving to clouds, "Come dance with me!"
The breeze sings soft, a lullaby sweet,
While roses debate who has the best seat.

Lilies prance, with grace so divine,
"Watch us bloom, beneath this sunshine!"
But snapdragons snicker, in quite the scene,
"We're the real stars, don't be so mean!"

In the Company of Blossoms

A garden party with blooms all around,
Tulips in tuxedos, all dressed up and bound.
"Who brought the snacks?" they eagerly ask,
As violets gossip, behind a green mask.

Daffodils dance, sharing jokes quite absurd,
"Why did the rose cross the path?" they purred.
To get to the garden, where laughter is free,
And everyone's petals flap joyfully!

The Allure of the Garden's Heart

In the heart of the garden, a scandal unfolds,
Where marigolds brag of their shimmering golds.
"I'm brighter than you!" a zinnia claims,
While ferns shake their heads, rolling their names.

Cacti chuckle, in corners they lay,
"We have sharp wit, come join the fray!"
As dandelions blow wishes with flair,
Creating mischief with petals in the air.

Whispers of Blooming Dreams

In the garden, gnomes do dance,
With tiny hats, they take a chance.
Rabbits wiggle, dresses two,
Chasing flowers, what a view!

Ladybugs wear coats of red,
Whisper secrets 'neath a bed.
Butterflies play hide and seek,
Tickled petals, laughter's peak.

Bees debate on who's the best,
Buzzing loudly, a lively fest.
Sunflowers argue, heads held high,
With pollen swords, they reach the sky.

While daisies twirl in gentle breeze,
Their giggles echo through the trees.
In this field of joyous schemes,
There's nothing quite like blooming dreams.

Veils of Fragrance in the Breeze

Jasmine winks with fragrant sighs,
As stinky socks scare off the flies.
Lavender laughs with a cheery hue,
Convincing daisies to join the crew.

Marigolds juggle, petals aflare,
While garden chairs start to declare:
'We ain't moving, oh what a fuss,
Let's just sit and talk to the bus!'

Sunflowers gossip with ants in tow,
About the gossip they just won't show.
A whiff of ivy, secretive tease,
Hiding laughter in the soft breeze.

As petals flutter, the breeze takes flight,
With all this mischief, what a delight!
In the garden, where tales arise,
Fragrance hides with mischievous eyes.

Chasing Colorful Shadows

Chasing shadows in fields of hue,
Rabbits don capes; who knew?
A snicker and giggle as colors blend,
Painted flowers begin to bend.

Crickets play cards, laying down deals,
While flower pots spin crazy wheels.
In this garden of jest and fun,
Silly shadows know no sun.

Dandelions dance, puffing with pride,
While sneaky violets try to hide.
The sunflowers shout, 'We're all in!'
Running from shadows, it's a win-win!

With petals spinning like tops in joy,
Every bloom's a playful toy.
Chasing laughter, never alone,
In this garden, mischief's grown.

The Language of Soft Blossoms

Whispering blooms have secrets to share,
In the garden where joy fills the air.
Tulips shout with colors so bright,
While pansies giggle in pure delight.

The daisies whisper, 'Look at the bee!'
Stumbling around, forgetting the tea.
A banquet of petals and sips of dew,
In this world of laughter, just me and you.

'What's in a name?' the roses cry,
As humorous bees buzz on by.
Tickled stems dressed up with flair,
In soft blossoms, jokes disappear.

The humor hides in the softest layer,
Nature's jesters, oh what a player!
In every bloom, a giggle resides,
This floral language, where laughter abides.

Secrets Beneath the Floral Canopy

In the garden where daisies gossip,
Laughter blooms with every twist.
Silly bees wear tiny hats,
While butterflies dance, how could they miss?

Sunflowers think they're all the rage,
Comparing heights, they stand in pride.
But that little weed with its cheeky face,
Says, "I'm the surprise in this flowery tide!"

Tulips gather for a tea,
Discussing who's the fairest bloom.
But the roses roll their eyes and say,
"We'll let the fragrance clear the room!"

Violets sneak in at midnight,
To crash the primrose's soirée.
Sipping dew from crystal cups,
Their antics brighten even the gray!

Dances of the Blooming Hearts

In tuxedo petals, roses twirl,
While daisies cheer, oh what a whirl!
The lilies laugh, not taking turns,
As bumblebees do their dances, and yearn.

Each flower has a secret move,
A waltz, a jig, a groove to prove.
The garden's a stage, lights aglow,
With a flower show that steals the show!

But when the wind makes branches sway,
The blooms collide, they shout, "Hooray!"
Mismatched petals hug and spin,
And all agree, it's fun to begin!

Then the moon peeks, teasingly bright,
Saying, "Join me for a dance tonight!"
They sway as one, a floral sight,
With giggles echoing into the twilight.

Mosaic of Nature's Whisper

A patchwork quilt of colors bright,
Whispers from the flowers take flight.
A dandelion finds it's quite a stunt,
To give the bees her fuzzy front!

Marigolds tell tales of yesterday,
While violets giggle at the fray.
Even daisies, shy and sweet,
Join in with a rhythm, oh so neat!

Buttercups, in golden glow,
Debate the best blooms—they steal the show!
But the humble clover, with a wink,
Says, "Hey folks, just stop and think!"

For all the hues and shapes galore,
Life's a laugh, with blooms to adore.
Nature's canvas, painted keen,
With every flower bright and green!

Awakened by Nature's Palette

As dawn unveils its brush of light,
Blossoms wake with sheer delight.
A sunflower yawns, sporting its grin,
While dew drops cheer, "Let's begin!"

The tulips giggle, just a tad shy,
Wondering if the clouds will fly.
But forget-me-nots play peek-a-boo,
"Here we are, come join the crew!"

A field of petals, what a sight,
They brainstorm ideas for the night.
With costumes made of leaves and grass,
Every flower hopes that fun will last!

Finally, as stars start to gleam,
The garden plots a midnight dream.
Nature's palette, full of glee,
Brings laughter wild, for all to see!

Paving Paths with Petals

In a garden of socks, I tripped on a shoe,
Daisy chains giggle, the daisies all knew.
Bumblebees buzzed, wearing tiny hats tight,
While a snail held a sign, 'Keep your paces light!'

The sun painted laughs on the petals so bright,
Rabbits on rollerblades zoomed left and right.
I followed the laughter, an unplanned parade,
While daisies teamed up for a grand charade.

Twirling with flowers, we danced through the grass,
Who knew that the daisies could all have such sass?
One winked at me with a charming allure,
Reminding me joy is the best kind of cure.

As nightfall approached, the moon said with glee,
"Let's stir up some mischief, just you wait and see!"
So together we plotted a funny grand scheme,
With petals on pathways, we'd reign like a dream!

Scented Reveries in Blooming Meadows

In meadows so silly, the flowers had tales,
Each bloom huddled close, sharing ticklish trails.
Butterflies giggled as they took their flights,
While squirrels in tuxedos played poker at nights.

A bumblebee buzzed with a musical flair,
He crooned 'Love Me Tender' to the fragrant air.
Lavender laughed as it swayed to the beat,
While daisies bright donned their floral retreat.

With daisies as pillows and violets as sheets,
They slumbered in peace, sharing sweet gummy treats.
But one curious flower, with dreams in its sights,
Plotted to prank all the butterflies' flights.

It wore a bright veil made of shimmering dew,
Leaving guests baffled, a comedy brew.
So in blooming meadows, let laughter abide,
For the essence of joy is the best flower guide!

Bursting into Colorful Whispers

In gardens of giggles, the roses wore shoes,
While tulips declared, "We don't follow the moos!"
The sunflowers danced, they twirled and spun,
Declaring that laughter is where the fun's won.

A lilac on drums beat a rhythm so snappy,
While poppies rejoiced, looking stylish and happy.
There's magic in colors, like a paintbrush gone wild,
In a duet of blossoms, each one like a child.

They painted the skies with hues of delight,
The violets were giggling from morning to night.
"Catch me if you can!" yelled the daisies with glee,
As they wobbled and tumbled, so carefree and free.

So amidst all the laughter, one flower took flight,
And spotted a squirrel in a costume that night.
With whispers of colors, joy danced all around,
In gardens of giggles, happiness found!

Floral Navigations of the Soul

Among petals of laughter, a journey began,
With roses as maps, and a sprightly old man.
He wore a fine shirt made of vibrant blooms,
And chuckled as dandelions banished their glooms.

Through pathways of saffron and paths paved in thyme,
He shared silly stories of each fragrant chime.
A daisy with glasses read poems at dawn,
While pansies in tuxedos hummed soft little songs.

Goldenrod gossip kept the breezes light,
As butterflies flitted, hearts full of delight.
"Let's sail on a breeze through this botanical trail,
With giggles and chuckles, we'll surely prevail!"

So onward they wandered, through gardens so vast,
With blossoms as markers, each moment a blast.
In floral adventures, the soul felt so free,
For laughter's the map, and joy's the decree!

Treading on Floral Fantasies

I slipped on daisies, what a sight,
Floral foes danced in the sunlight.
A rose yelled, "Watch where you tread!"
I said, "Just trying to see the spread!"

A dandelion laughed right in my face,
"You're losing the race; this isn't a chase!"
I tripped on some clover, the giggles flew,
"Watch your step, buddy, we're laughing at you!"

Sunflowers chuckled, tall and bright,
"Your dancing skills? A true delight!"
I bowed to my fans, gave it a twirl,
But stumbled back, oh what a whirl!

Yet in this garden where humor blooms,
We all laugh together, avoiding the gloom.
So bring on the laughter, let joy overflow,
In this silly wonderland, we steal the show!

Echoes of Garden Hues

In a garden bright, hues dance and sway,
Petunias tease with their vibrant display.
A lily leaned in, whispered with glee,
"Hey, did you hear? I'm the 'belle' of the spree!"

A tulip tripped, oh what a scene,
Splashed bright colors, what could it mean?
"My style's the best!" it declared with flair,
While roses rolled their eyes in the air.

A daffodil stood, proud and aloof,
"No one can top my golden proof!"
But bees just buzzed, saying, "Oh please,
We love them all, with such silly ease!"

As petals laugh in the warm summer light,
This garden of hues ignites pure delight.
Through chortles and giggles, truth does emerge,
United in laughter, we dance and surge!

Serenade of Delicate Layers

In a field of layers, each bloom seems to sing,
Forget about worries, let the flowers fling.
A daisy quipped, 'I'm the crown jewel here,'
While marigolds giggled, spreading their cheer.

Tall sunflowers waved as if to confer,
"Let's play a game, who's the best bloomer?"
A shy little orchid began to sway,
"Hurry up friends, before I decay!"

A bumblebee buzzed, all chubby and round,
"Who needs a crown when joy can surround?"
With laughter and shades, our frivolous play
Brought giggles aplenty, chasing blues away!

Among these layers, where joy intertwines,
Every bloom's quirky, each story aligns.
A harmony found, let the fun resonate,
In nature's embrace, we celebrate fate!

In the Realm of Verdant Dreams

In the green expanse where the crazy vines grow,
A cabbage called out, 'Hey, don't steal my show!'
While carrots were blushing, they shyly agreed,
"This leafy parade's got quite the breed!"

A radish exclaimed, full of zest and delight,
"Come dance in my kingdom, it feels just right!"
As spinach spun round in a velvety whirl,
"Flaunt your green shades, give nature a twirl!"

Tomatoes were giggling, blushing so red,
"Is it time for a feast?" they eagerly said.
The lettuce just chuckled, "I'll keep it all cool,
Together we rule this green leafy school!"

In our verdant dreams where laughter collides,
Each plant is a friend, and joy never hides.
We frolic together, in sunshine and scheme,
A world of green whispers, "Let's follow that dream!"

The Resonance of Nature's Palette

In gardens where the bugs do dance,
A daisy wore its underpants.
A rose once tried to tell a joke,
But thorns just made the laughter choke.

With colors splashed like paint gone wild,
The sunflowers smirk, so bright, so styled.
Lilies giggle in their proud attire,
Their fragrance rivals a nearby fire.

The violets plan a prank on bees,
But buzzing's just too hard to tease.
While petals flap in breezy cheer,
Nature's laugh, we hold so dear.

In this serene botanical spree,
The flowers nod, 'Come dance with me!'
And in this bloom, the fun won't fade,
A garden joke, a grand charade.

Blooming in the Canvas of Time

A tulip dressed in polka dots,
Complains of pests that steal her pots.
The daisies shout, 'Just look at me!'
While winking at their people-free.

Cornflowers keep an artist's brush,
As raindrops fall in quite a rush.
A bold petunia wears a crown,
While birds applaud from up and down.

The daisies hold an art critique,
Declaring dullness is quite meek.
With all this flair, who wouldn't cheer?
In blooms like these, there's fun to steer.

So let's create a wild bouquet,
Where nature paints with laughter's play!
In every hue and splendid line,
A garden's giggle marks the time.

Songs of the Unfurling

Beneath the sun, the buds all chat,
A crocus jokes, 'I'm not just that!'
While daffodils boast with a grin,
'In spring, we all shed our winter skin!'

Tulips form a raucous band,
Their melodies both bold and grand.
The lilacs hum a silly tune,
As bumblebees join with a swoon.

In this flowered circus, oh so bright,
Petals twirl in a dazzling sight.
The blossoms sing of sunlit days,
With laughter dancing through the rays.

So blossom forth with mirth and cheer,
For nature's joke is crystal clear.
With each unfurling, let us sway,
In rhythm with the blooms at play.

Aromatic Adventures of the Heart

In a garden full of fragrant fun,
The jasmine whispers, 'I'm number one!'
Mint jokes, 'I'm cool, just like I seem,'
As rosemary adds, 'I'm quite the dream!'

Chrysanthemums bring their playful flair,
While lilacs tease the breeze in air.
'Why do we smell so wonderfully?'
The daisies giggle, 'Just wait and see!'

With citrus scents on every path,
The garden's laughter sparks a math.
While petals tickle noses wide,
In heady aromas, joy will reside.

So dance amidst the blooms so bright,
Where aromatic hearts take flight.
In laughter's scent, we find our art,
In every flower beats a heart.

Chrysanthemums and Midnight Dreams

In the garden, when night creeps,
Chrysanthemums dance, giggling heaps.
They sway to the tune of the moonlit rays,
Whispering secrets in funny ways.

Bugs in tuxedos join in with flair,
While frogs in caps croak without a care.
A symphony of laughter fills the air,
As dreaming flowers create a rare stare.

When shadows play hide and seek anew,
The cosmos chuckles, sharing a view.
In their soft petals, dreams are spun,
Carnival laughter under the sun.

With every bloom, the night grows bright,
A parade of whimsy in soft twilight.
In chrysanthemum costumes, they twirl and shine,
Creating a joke that's simply divine.

The Heartbeat of Nature's Blooms

The blossoms pulse like a drum so sweet,
While bees groove to the buzzing beat.
Daisy's got rhythm, flaunts her style,
With tulips spinning in a floral aisle.

The roses chuckle with perfumed grace,
While arriving bees do a funny chase.
Nature's heartbeat, a lively dance,
In this garden, everyone takes a chance.

Snapdragons snap in a playful jest,
As bumblebees join, dressed in their best.
Here blooms a riot, a raucous show,
Where petals throw jokes, and the laughter blows.

In the heart of the garden, joy takes hold,
A tapestry woven with stories told.
As flowers pulse and giggle aloud,
Nature's blooms wear their fun so proud.

Fragrant Footprints of the Heart

Through fields I tread with a silly grin,
Following scents where the fun begins.
Each step a story, every twist a sigh,
With the sun on my face, I leap and fly.

Lilies laugh softly, waving their flair,
While daisies whisper secrets in the air.
Petunias nudge me with pink, cheeky glee,
As I dance through the blossoms, feeling so free.

With fragrant footprints, let's leave a trail,
Collecting giggles like a clever tale.
Every bloom's a memory waiting to write,
A comedy skit under the sunlight.

So twirl with the blossoms, let laughter spark,
In this whimsical journey, there's no time to park.
With petals of joy and scents so bright,
We chase funny footprints into the night.

Marigold Memories on the Wind

Marigolds wink as the breeze rolls in,
Spreading laughter where joy is a sin.
With every gust, their giggles bloom,
As memories swirl like a colorful plume.

Under the sun's watchful, funny gaze,
The marigolds share their fragrant arrays.
Each petal a tale, a chuckle, a song,
In this silly garden, where hearts belong.

The wind carries whispers, silly and sweet,
Of marigold parties with fairies that greet.
Each moment a dance, every turn a cheer,
In the garden of joy, there's nothing to fear.

So chase the marigold memories afar,
As they twirl with the daisies, like a bright shooting star.
Let the wind be your guide, and laughter your aim,
In this world of flowers, we all play the game.

The Magic of Blooming Minutes

In a garden filled with giggles,
Laughter mingles with the breeze,
Flowers dance in silly wiggles,
While bees buzz in perfect tease.

Butterflies in costume prance,
Wearing stripes that clash and clash,
They all join the merry dance,
As daisies break into a bash!

A sunflower dons a hat,
Tipped at a jaunty angle wide,
While tulips chat about the cat,
Who thinks he's their secret guide.

Time here blooms, a joyful trick,
Every moment wraps a joke,
In this space, we're all so quick,
To smile at life's delightful poke!

Sunlit Paths of the Blossoming Soul

Under the sun, the tulips tease,
With colors that shout, 'Look at me!'
They sway with the tiniest breeze,
In a game of hide and seek, whee!

Daisies wear their sunny crowns,
Winking at the wandering bees,
While snails slide in tiny gowns,
Claiming victory with such ease.

The path is paved with scattered laughs,
While squirrels perform their silly shows,
In nature's theater, it's fun in halves,
As shadows dance where sunlight flows.

Every step a secret giggle,
As we wander and break into cheer,
Magical moments make us wiggle,
In paths where joy is always near!

The Garden of Forgotten Wishes

In a garden where dreams collide,
Forgotten wishes sprout and bloom,
With whimsy dancing side by side,
They fill the air with sweet perfume.

A gnome wearing mismatched socks,
Hides behind a bush of thyme,
While fairies play with stylish locks,
Creating chaos, oh so prime!

We find requests from long ago,
Stuck in between the leaves so green,
Like 'Please, oh please, let rivers flow',
And 'Can I have a jelly bean?'

Here in this patch of joy and jest,
Laughter lingers in every nook,
Where silly dreams, they never rest,
And wishes hide in every book!

Threads of Eden in Every Step

Every footfall weaves a tale,
On the path where flowers speak,
With colors bright that never pale,
And whispers of the roaming creek.

A rabbit hops in mismatched shoes,
With carrots tucked in every pocket,
While squirrels wear goggles, can you choose?
To join the fun? Just come and rock it!

As daisies share their secret rhymes,
With jokes that tickle even trees,
We dance to nature's silly chimes,
Each moment's filled with summer's tease.

In the canvas of this vibrant ground,
We paint our joy with laughter's thread,
In every step, a joy profound,
Where Eden blooms, and smiles are spread!

The Dance of Spring's Caress

The flowers sway with playful grace,
As bees do dance, a buzzing race.
They flirt with colors, bold and bright,
A comedy in morning light.

The daisies giggle, tulips tease,
While blossoms play in the gentle breeze.
They whisper secrets, laugh and sing,
In nature's stage, they are the kings.

The gardener trips, a trowel flies,
His plants conspire, oh what a guise!
A flower's prickle, a bee's surprise,
He leaves the scene with wide-eyed sighs.

Yet springtime's charm is oh-so-sweet,
With blooms that twirl on tiny feet.
In every petal, joy resides,
A jolly romp where cheer abides.

Fluttering Dreams Among the Blooms

In fields of vibrant, swirling hues,
Butterflies flaunt their funny shoes.
They flit and flutter, with such delight,
Wearing patterns that are out of sight.

The bumblebees wear tiny hats,
While ladybugs are playing bats.
A garden party, wild and free,
Where worms perform a wiggly spree.

The roses jest, with prickly jokes,
While daisies giggle, sharing pokes.
Each bloom a character, on display,
As nature's laughter steals the day.

But watch your step, oh unsuspecting,
For ants are planning their perfect wrecking.
A bloom of mirth, a swirl of cheer,
In each petal, a chuckle or sneer.

Beneath the Blooming Canopy

Beneath the blooms, a shady show,
A gathering of friends in a row.
They share their stories, wild and grand,
In petals bright, they take a stand.

The lilacs whisper tales of sass,
While hyacinths spill secrets en masse.
Each flower cracks a clever quip,
As the sun kisses the blossoms' tip.

A butterfly photobombs the squad,
With antics that are quite the façade.
The crocus rolls its leafy eyes,
While tulips snicker, oh what a prize!

In this assembly, laughter grows,
Where nature's humor freely flows.
Amidst the colors, joy's displayed,
In bloom's embrace, the world's arrayed.

Echoes of Floral Journeys

On this path of floral trails,
Petals carry cheeky tales.
Each bloom a story, bright and bold,
Of sunny days and mischief told.

The violets hum a cheerful tune,
While snapdragons act like a cartoon.
Their silly poses, a sight to see,
In the garden's wild jubilee.

The sunflowers strut with heads held high,
While dandelions blow wishes to the sky.
In the garden, giggles take their flight,
As bees play tag, from morn till night.

An echo of laughter fills the air,
With every sway, Every vibrant flare.
In every petal's soft caress,
The humor of nature we must confess.

Blossoms and the Art of Letting Go

A bouquet once filled with cheer,
Now sits with dust, oh dear!
Roses used to dance and sway,
Now they just wish for the day.

I tossed a petal, what a sight,
It fluttered off into the night.
It landed on a snail, oh wow,
Now they're best friends somehow!

All the daisies rolled their eyes,
While lilies planned their great surprise.
They whispered soft, with much delight,
"Was that a petal? Oh, what a flight!"

So here's to blooms and breaking free,
To petals lost, wine made from tea.
Let laughter grow in every row,
In gardens wild, let the humor flow!

Garden of Whispered Wishes

In a garden where wishes bloom,
I found a gnome in a bright costume.
He claimed to plant a wishing tree,
But it turned out to be a weed, you see!

Butterflies laughed, sipping on dew,
While the daisies revealed their latest coup.
"Dear honeybee, you've missed a spot!"
"Buzz off," said bee, "This place is hot!"

The sunflowers yawned, and then they spun,
Chasing shadows, saying it's all in fun.
"Who needs wishes when you can play?
Just skip the chores and dance today!"

With wishes fluttering in the breeze,
The garden chuckled with such ease.
So here's to laughter, bright and loud,
In a world where whimsy is allowed!

Romantic Vistas of the Floral Realm

Oh, the roses set a romantic scene,
But thorns are sneaky and quite mean!
A daisy tried to woo a bee,
But he just buzzed—"Not for me!"

"I love you like the sun loves rain,"
Said one bloom, while it felt the pain.
The violets in shadows threw a tease,
"Dating flowers? Oh, if you please!"

Tulips blushed with varying hues,
While petals whispered all their blues.
One flower sighed, "Let's morph and twist,
Romance is hard, I can't resist!"

But love around took a funny spin,
Where sun and shade did chase a grin.
So raise a toast with nectar sweet,
In this floral court, we can all compete!

Starlight over the Blooming Fields

Under starlit skies, the daisies play,
With promise of mischief, night turns to day.
"Let's tell the moon a silly tale,"
Said one tiny bud, "Let's go, don't fail!"

Then tulips giggled, they couldn't resist,
"Shh! Don't wake the bees; they'll raise a fist!"
Frolicking blooms, what a sight to see,
As daisies planned a grand jubilee!

They danced with shadows, dipped into dreams,
Running with laughter and whimsical themes.
"Hold on tight, we'll twirl and glide,
In the starlit night, we'll surely ride!"

So here in the fields, with stars aglow,
Plants spread joy, as breezes blow.
With night's embrace, they will not tire,
For blooming fun is their heart's desire!

Unfolding Stories of the Flowering Souls

In the garden where flowers giggle,
Bees don't buzz, they dance and wiggle.
A rose tried to tell a joke once,
But thorns got in the way of the puns.

Lilies wear hats made of dew,
While daisies sing out something new.
A sunbeam slips, playing tag with the breeze,
But gets tangled in stubborn trees.

Tulips compete in a silly race,
Hopping around with blooms on their face.
They slip and tumble, it's quite absurd,
Claiming the title of the quickest flowered bird.

So gather round and listen up,
To tales of petals, smiles, and hiccup.
Among the blossoms, life's a jest,
Where every flower laughs at the rest.

Treading on Fragile Colors

Waltzing on colors, oh what a sight,
Who knew daisies could dance through the night?
With every misstep, a new shade appears,
As tulips laugh, but hold back their tears.

Butterflies prance in formal attire,
Pollen confetti, they never tire.
"Watch out for me!" a rose shouts loud,
But stepped on a snail, oh how he's cowed.

The violets giggle at their own clumsiness,
"Let's flip and flop, who cares if we mess?"
Every color smirks at the tripping crew,
With each twist and tumble, they burst out anew.

Fall back to earth, they all just collide,
But tangled in petals, they'll always abide.
In this crazy dance, they set the tone,
For laughter and joy in their color-blown zone.

Hues of the Heart's Garden

In the garden of feelings, where colors collide,
Silly sunflowers grow, filled with pride.
Each one shouts, "I'm the best, can't you see?"
But the daisies whisper, "Just let us be!"

A cactus joins in, feeling rather bold,
"Who needs softness? I'm prickly gold!"
While peonies blush, thinking they're shy,
They giggle at jokes from a passing butterfly.

The garden's a riot, a bustling fair,
Where every hue tells tales of despair.
Then blossoms erupt in laughter so sweet,
As bumbles and hiccups turn into a treat.

So wander through feelings, whimsical and bright,
As petals laugh hard in the soft morning light.
For in this odd garden, chaos holds sway,
And hues of the heart have a funny ballet.

Nature's Soft Embrace

Under a tree, where shadows play,
Nature gives a hug, in a quirky way.
The bush giggles, tickling your sides,
While squirrels scamper and take joyrides.

Flowers wave hello, with stems like arms,
Engaging the breeze in their fragrant charms.
"Catch us if you can!" the petals declare,
While dandelions puff like they don't care.

Grass blades chatter, gossiping away,
Making jokes 'til the end of the day.
A butterfly flaps with a playful tone,
"It's all a race, but I'm flying alone!"

So join in the fun, let petals lead on,
In nature's embrace, worries are gone.
For laughter is found where blossoms entwine,
In this shimmering place, feeling splendidly fine.

Lullabies of the Flourishing

In gardens where daisies dance,
Bees buzz around like they're in a trance.
A squirrel steals a shoe, how absurd!
Nature's antics are truly unheard.

Balloons float high, tied to a bloom,
While giggling gnomes sweep up the room.
Silly frogs sing out of tune,
Chasing after butterflies that swoon.

Voyages Through Verdant Valleys

A snail races fast, or so it seems,
Competing with a frog who just dreams.
They slip and slide on leaves so slick,
Nature's a circus; it's quite a trick!

There's a tree that juggles fruit all day,
While birds play games, in their own way.
A picnic turns into a dance party,
With ants serving cake, oh, so hearty!

Whispers of the Nature's Canvas

In forests where the trunks wear hats,
Witty rabbits make jokes with their chats.
A butterfly sneezes, colors abound,
Painting the flowers all over the ground.

With worms debating who's the best dancer,
They wiggle and squirm, double the chancer.
At dusk, fireflies put on a show,
Lighting up the stage; go, butterflies, go!

Mosaic of Whispers and Blossoms

In a patch of blooms, a frog sits bold,
Swapping tales with the marigold.
While moths play tag, sparking delight,
A blossom brushes off a bee's slight flight.

The daisies giggle, a comedic feat,
As dandelions scatter like confetti sweet.
And with each wind gust, the laughter grows,
Nature's grand play without any prose.

Enchanted by the Aroma of Life

In gardens bright, the flowers dance,
With scents so strong, they seem to prance.
A bee took flight, quite unprepared,
It buzzed so loud, the cat just stared.

Amidst the blooms, a snail crawls slow,
Wearing a hat, it's quite the show.
Mice in hats steal seeds to munch,
While squirrels giggle, they'll never hunch.

A dandelion made wishes sprout,
Until the wind came blowing out.
The birthday cake of petals torn,
A feast for bees, the party's worn.

In this wild mix, a rose went red,
With dreams of cream cheese, it has said.
A flower's quest, both weird and wild,
With laughs aplenty, just like a child.

Symphony of Botanical Journeys

The daisies gossip in the breeze,
Complaining 'bout the bumblebees.
A marigold responds quite bold,
"At least we don't have tales retold!"

In every pot, a cactus sighs,
Wishing it had sweeter pies.
As weeds croon their rebellious song,
"Why do we always get it wrong?"

A sunflower beams, so tall and proud,
While violets hide beneath a cloud.
They trade their tales of sun and rain,
In their own wacky floral lane.

A lilac dreams of days in spring,
Imitating birds that love to sing.
With petals waving like a wave,
They'll charm those who dare to brave.

Whispers of Blossom

In morning light, the buds awake,
A tulip's giggle causes a quake.
The wind joins in with a silly twist,
As daisies laugh and can't resist.

A daffodil wears a jaunty hat,
While roses ponder, 'What's up with that?'
The crocus trips over its own stem,
Plant life drama, a grand mayhem.

A trellis squeaks, what a noisy tale,
As geraniums set out to sail.
A petunia sighs, "Where's my tea?"
While lilacs spill their secrets with glee.

The hibiscus twirls in a sunny whirl,
Declaring life's the sweetest pearl.
In the garden's laughter, we find delight,
With every bud that bursts in light.

Fragrance of Desire

Sweet scent of life wafts through the air,
As flowers vow to boldly share.
A daisy winks at passing bees,
Whispering, "Come dance with such ease!"

Lilies prance in patterned gowns,
While clovers giggle, losing frowns.
Tulips play hide-and-seek at dusk,
With petals soft, it's just a must!

The jasmine dreams of moonlit nights,
Where fragrant kisses brings delights.
A sunflower tries to strike a pose,
But with its roots, it just froze!

As petals twirl 'neath the stars so bright,
The garden hums with sheer delight.
With every sway, and twist of charm,
Life's fragrance swirls, it stays warm.

Chasing Shadows of Spring

A daisy danced with a cheeky grin,
While tulips whispered secrets of sin.
A bee in a bow tie buzzed by fast,
Claiming he's the king of the flowered cast.

The daffodils giggled, 'What a sight!'
As they plotted to steal the warm sunlight.
While pansies played cards, oh what a game,
'We'll bet on the rain! It's all the same.'

Caterpillar crawls with a sip of tea,
Laughing at flowers attempting to flee.
They dodge the big foot of a clumsy dog,
While avoiding the squishy mud like a hog.

Joyfully now, the buds come to play,
Drawing out laughter in a bright bouquet.
So, who needs a king when you've got a show,
In gardens where giggles and whimsy grow?

The Lure of Blossoms on Breeze

A lily looked up with a curious sigh,
'Why do petals always flutter and fly?'
They whispered of dreams in the warm afternoon,
And twirled in the light like a cartoon.

The roses conspired their bright petals spill,
'Let's create a whirl with a daffodil!'
Wind waltzed them close, what a funny scene,
As petals twisted like a dance machine.

Amazing aromas from blossoms in flight,
Made every bee giggle with pure delight.
While a squirrel juggled nuts on a stem,
The flowers applauded, 'You're our gem!'

Breezy ballet with a splash of good cheer,
Each blossom echoed laughter near and dear.
Through blossoms they raced, oh what a tease,
In a world of giggles, carried by breeze.

Where Flowers Speak in Silence

In a quiet corner, blooms start to chat,
With whispers of sunshine and the tip of a hat.
'Did you see that bee looking oh-so proud?'
They laughed in colors, vibrant and loud.

The violets chuckled, their secrets to share,
'That bug just fell; it's a comedy fair!'
Chrysanthemums nod as they sip on dew,
'What a clumsy ballet, who knew bugs flew?'

Lilies applaud as the wind takes a bow,
They tease at the clouds that are fluffing like now.
Sammy the snail, he slipped on a leaf,
'Oh dear, that's the epitome of grief!'

Yet laughter erupts with the dawn of the day,
These flowers, of course, have their whimsical way.
In silence, they giggle at life's little jest,
A garden of chuckles; they know it best.

Blossoms Under a Canvas Sky

Under the canvas, where colors collide,
Flowers unfold with a whimsical pride.
A sunflower snapped and a tulip just spun,
They giggled and joked, oh what fun, what fun!

Daisies held court, their judgment so sweet,
'Who's wearing the wildest blossom on their seat?'
The zinnias roared, 'We've got a surprise!
A bumblebee with glasses, oh what a prize!'

Paint-splashed petals on a breeze-driven quest,
Each bloom with a story, they're truly the best.
They danced in the sunlight with style and grace,
Gritty little weeds joined the joyful race.

With pollen confetti falling from above,
They twirled in the laughter, the glory of love.
So here's to the blossoms under the sky,
Where joy takes root, and spirits fly high!

Captivated by Nature's Elegance

In a garden full of flowers so bright,
The tulips dance in the teasing light.
Bumblebees buzz with their tiny flair,
While daisies sway without a care.

The roses whisper secrets at noon,
"Don't forget your honey, you silly baboon!"
Butterflies giggle, flapping with glee,
As they race past soon-to-be honeybee.

The sunflowers stand tall, trying to boast,
But I just want toast and the perfect roast.
They're proud of their height, but who really cares?
I'd rather play tag with the vegetable pairs.

Among scents of lilacs and grasses so lush,
I'm chased by a squirrel; he's got quite the rush.
With critters around, the laughter ignites,
In this whimsical world, joy takes flight.

Radiance of the Wandering Heart

Oh, the daisies tease with their cheer-filled grins,
While squirrels play poker, betting their sins.
"Your acorns are safe, don't worry, dear friend!"
But the wind whispers loudly, "This has to end!"

Chasing after the sun like a kid with a kite,
Petunias start gossiping, causing a fright.
With a giggle and twirl, they plot their next game,
I'm off on adventures, with joy as my aim.

The pansies pluck jokes from the air with finesse,
While I skip past the pond in my best, silliest dress.
With frogs croaking humor, they join in the fun,
Nature's a party, come join everyone!

Amidst bursts of laughter, I twirl and I sway,
With petals as confetti, come dance, come play!
The wildflowers chuckle, "Oh, what a delight!"
As I trip over roots in the soft, golden light.

Floral Reverie Under Starlit Skies

Starry nights in the garden, oh what a sight,
The moon's casting shadows, all fluffy and white.
With a daisy as my hat, I dance on the lawn,
While the tulips hold hands, like a floral bonbon.

Crickets are crooning their jazz with great flair,
Frogs in the background are quite debonair.
"Hop here and there, shimmy left and right!"
Catch me if you can, I'll twirl out of sight.

The night air's alive with laughter and cheer,
While fireflies join in, their lights oh so near.
A daffodil giggles, "Oh, what a fine bash!"
As we waltz through the darkness, a colorful splash!

When the stars twinkle bright, and dreams dance in view,
Nature treats us to laughs, and joy ever true.
So join this madcap floral serenade,
Under the cosmic quilt, our laughter cascades.

Chronicles of the Garden's Secrets

In the heart of the garden, where silliness brews,
Bees wear tiny hats, while flowers amuse.
Each blossom has tales that they softly tell,
Of garden escapades, oh, can you dwell?

Violets conspire, "Let's prank the old snail!"
"Just watch how he moves, this'll never fail!"
The sunflowers giggle, "We'll keep score,"
While the roses cheer, "Let's give him more!"

An epic of laughter, and mischief unfolds,
As lilies throw shade, and the petunias scold.
"Don't trip on the roots, you clumsy old leaf!"
Echoes of chuckles, a garden's belief.

So here's to the flora, the quirks and the zany,
In the chronicles told, life is not rainy.
For every small bud has a story to share,
In the whimsical garden, laughter fills the air.

A Journey Through Fragrant Pathways

In a garden so bright, I took a wrong turn,
Found bees wearing hats, oh the lessons I learned.
They danced all around in a buzz and a spin,
Swatting flies off their suits, like they're trying to win.

A squirrel in a vest, with a camera in hand,
Snapped selfies with daisies, all part of the plan.
The roses were grinning, waving their leaves,
While lilacs were gossiping under their eaves.

The daisies played poker, the tulips kept score,
As the gardener yelled, "Hey, no games on my floor!"
Her watering can spouted the light of the sun,
Turns out flowers just want to have plenty of fun.

I left with a chuckle, a story to share,
Of flowers in fancy, and plants full of flair.
Next time you wander through gardens so bright,
Take a laugh on the trail, and enjoy the delight.

Threads of Life in Bloom

A patchwork of hues in a quilt of delight,
Stitching sunflowers, daisies, oh what a sight!
With threads made of giggles, they fashion their cheer,
Padding themselves with the jokes they hold dear.

Zinnias wore glasses, and pansies stood tall,
They debated the best way to grow at the mall.
Frangipani said, "I prefer naps in the sun,"
While peonies chuckled, "Oh wait, we just run!"

The daisies created a rhythm so sweet,
As butterflies danced to their tap-tap-tap feet.
The violets in chorus sang songs of old,
While grasses turned green, feeling ever so bold.

With laughter and joy sewn into each seam,
These floral companions fulfilled every dream.
So let your heart bloom with mirth without end,
Amongst the fabric of life, you will always blend.

Blossoms in the Twilight

As dusk draped the garden, the flowers took flight,
Under twinkling stars, they sparkled so bright.
The marigolds giggled, playing hide and seek,
While lilacs recited the latest flower sneak peek.

The tulips were tangoing, kicking up dust,
With a daffodil DJ, it was surely a must.
Roses were waltzing, they just couldn't stop,
While petunias hosted a wild rooftop flop.

The evening was filled with the sweetest of tunes,
As the moon threw a party, inviting the goons.
Violets dropped pop quizzes on all, what a sight!
Turns out flowers are clever, especially at night.

When the dawn made its entrance, the flowers retired,
With whispers of laughter and joy they conspired.
So next time you wander, don't miss the fun,
For blossoms at twilight shine brighter than one.

Fluttering Among the Floral Voices

In fields of bright colors, they gathered one day,
The blooms had a meeting, all ready to play.
A sunflower spoke loud, "Let's all spread the word!"
While daisies and daisies shouted back, absurd.

"Let's paint the blue sky with petals so free!"
A daffodil shouted, "Make room for me!"
The rest of the flowers erupted in glee,
Creating a symphony of color, you see.

Their chatter was wild, their joy uncontained,
With laughter and dance, they all felt unchained.
The lilacs mixed scents with a zesty perfume,
While orchids devised a delightful costume.

So when next you wander, and hear them discuss,
The humor in gardens is fit for all of us.
Join in their antics, let spirit imbue,
For among floral voices, there's always something new.

Threads of Blossom and Breeze

In a garden where daisies wear a bow,
Bees dance like they're at a show.
Then a ladybug chases a bumbling bee,
Sipping nectar, laughing with glee.

A butterfly flits, lost in its game,
As tulips tease, calling its name.
'Catch me if you can!' the flowers did shout,
While ants form a line, giggling about.

Caught in a breeze, a daffodil swayed,
Humor in blooms, no plans ever laid.
A stag beetle plays tag with a snail,
Laughing out loud, they follow a trail.

So come join the fun, plant your feet here,
In threads of laughter, let's share some cheer.
For flowers may wilt, but joy will remain,
In vibrant blooms where we play again.

The Enchantment of Floral Trails

On a quest for petals, a gnome took flight,
Riding a butterfly, oh what a sight!
He sought golden petals to weave a fine hat,
But stumbled upon a mad, dancing cat.

The scent of roses tickled his nose,
He sneezed so loud that the garden froze.
While sunflowers giggled, their faces aglow,
They plotted a prank, as soft breezes blow.

With pollen on fingers and dirt on his toes,
The gnome created a hiccup-filled pose.
The daisies yelled, "We need a parade!"
So arm-in-arm, they danced, unafraid.

In floral trails where laughter ignites,
Bumbles and giggles soar to new heights.
The gnome raised his hands, declared with a grin,
"Let's bloom where we laugh; let the fun begin!"

Petal-Bound Adventures

A snail on a quest, slow as a breeze,
Dreamed of adventures, just wanted to tease.
Said to a flower, "How far can we go?"
The flower replied, "We'll just grow and grow!"

They gathered a crew of curious bugs,
Who cheered and laughed, and gave silly hugs.
Before long, a fiesta broke out.
With ladybugs dancing while crickets sang loud!

Hop on a leaf, they rode down the stream,
Splashing in puddles, a whimsical dream.
With each turn they took, a giggle or two,
From bees wearing hats to ants with a stew.

Oh, the laughter that echoed through nature's embrace,
As they chased butterflies, at a reckless pace.
Adventure is sweet, with friends by your side,
In a world full of blooms, let your heart take a ride!

Transient Beauty in the Morning Light

Morning light kisses the petals so bright,
A daffodil giggles with pure delight.
The sun yawns wide, a sleepy old cat,
Chasing shadows, where mischief is at.

Blooming in color, a cheeky rose grins,
While a peony dangles from over its sins.
"Wanna play tag?" in the morning they ask,
"Mornings are fleeting; let's make joy our task!"

A forget-me-not whispers, "Oh what a thrill,
Don't let the dew drop; let's climb up the hill!"
So flowers all gathered, in vibrant array,
Chasing the sun, in their own goofy way.

Yet each blooming laughter fades slow in the light,
A reminder that fun may be brief, but it's bright.
So dance while you can, in this garden so grand,
For transient beauty holds joy in its hand.

The Dance of Colors in Moonlight

In the garden under the moon's glow,
Dancing flowers put on a show.
They sway and twirl in silly delight,
Even the daisies join in for the night.

A tulip trips over its own stem,
While rosettes giggle, it's a real gem.
Laughter echoes, bright hues collide,
Nature's revelry, no need to hide!

The violets can't keep their petals neat,
Whirling and twirling in a floral beat.
As the breeze chuckles and whispers loud,
Nature's party draws quite a crowd!

When the sun peeks in, the fun must wane,
Flowers doze off, it's time for the gain.
But wait till the night, they'll bloom once more,
For moonlight's magic, they're ready to soar!

Nectar of Unspoken Longings

Bumblebees buzz with secret dreams,
Over blossoms, they create teams.
One flirts with a tulip, so sweetly shy,
While daisies roll their eyes and sigh.

Hummingbirds hover, so full of grace,
Spilling nectar in a merry race.
'I'm just here for the sugar, no love,' they tease,
Meanwhile, roses blush in a gentle breeze.

Petunias gossip in tendril whispers,
About lost loves and late-night blisters.
'Did you see that bee? He tried to impress!'
All the blooms giggle in floral finesse.

With every sip, they plot and plan,
Chasing loves that can't quite span.
Yet nectar's sweet, so none can complain,
In this garden, joy is their refrain!

Delicate Threads of Nature's Artistry

Spiders weave webs with utmost pride,
Complaining that moths won't abide.
'Just look at my craft!' they spin and dart,
While the flowers giggle at their fine art.

Butterflies frolic, playing dress-up bright,
Swapping hues under the playful light.
'That shade's so last season,' the marigold grins,
As the blooms whisper of their floral wins.

Caterpillars munch, with pure delight,
'Not my fault, this diet's just right!'
They laugh at the daisies, all puffed and prude,
While sniffing at greens — how utterly rude!

But when evening falls, the stars will align,
Colors will fade, but spirits will shine.
For nature's fun is a timeless spree,
In this garden where all are carefree!

From Bud to Bloom: Life's Journey

In the morning, buds peek with glee,
Sipping dew, full of jubilee.
But wait, oh no! Was that a bee?
'Stand still, friends, we can't let them see!'

As the sun climbs, the blooms unfold,
Tales of adventure, yet to be told.
Some stretch their petals, a dazzling spread,
While others just nap, like a flowerbed.

Catching rays, they giggle and shine,
Chasing dandelions that joke they're divine.
Life is a whirl, a twist and a leap,
'Growing up's tough, can we just sleep?'

But as twilight dims and shadows entice,
The night brings dreams, all charming and nice.
From bud to bloom, in laughter they grow,
Life's a wild ride, let the fun flow!

www.ingramcontent.com/pod-product-compliance
Lightning Source LLC
Chambersburg PA
CBHW071822160426
43209CB00003B/164